AFV ALPHABET

RUSSELL PHILLIPS

SHILKA PUBLISHING

CONTENTS

INTRODUCTION

Inspired by Tim Gow's A to Z of Wargaming series of posts, I wrote an "A to Z" series of blog posts around the theme of AFVs (Armoured Fighting Vehicles). To mark History Writers Day 2022, I've edited the posts and collated them into this free book.

History Writers Day is a virtual Twitter Christmas Market for history-related books, both fiction and non-fiction. It's organised by @Books2Cover, which is well worth a follow if you don't do so already.

— RUSSELL PHILLIPS

A: ANTONOV A-40

When I started writing this series, I hoped to find some interesting subjects. I think it's fair to say that the Antonov A-40 flying tank qualifies as interesting. Airborne troops can be vulnerable, because they can't use heavy support weapons or vehicles. The A-40 was an attempt to address this problem, and provide them with some armoured support. The Soviet Union had previously experimented with dropping vehicles by parachute, but was not satisfied with this method, since the crews had to be dropped separately, and may land some distance from their vehicle.

The A-40 was a T-60 light tank with the addition of glider wings, fuselage and tail. Only one flight was attempted, in September 1942, during which the towing aircraft had to release the glider early, due to excessive drag. The glider was flown down to the ground without any problems, and after removing the glider attachments, the tank was driven back to base. Although the tank did fly and land safely, the idea was dropped. Eventually, the Soviet Union managed to perfect dropping BMDs by parachute with their crews inside.

B: BISHOP

During the western desert campaign in the early part of World War II, the British were impressed by the German self-propelled guns, and decided that they needed something similar. A requirement was issued for a self-propelled 25 pounder gun-howitzer. By August 1941 a prototype was ready, which had a simple boxy superstructure on top of a Valentine tank chassis. An order was placed for 100 vehicles, although the vehicle didn't impress crews in theatre. The superstructure was very large, making it an obvious target, and the gun had limited elevation, limiting its range to about half that of the towed version. The choice of an infantry tank hull meant that it was also rather slow.

No further orders were placed, and all the existing vehicles were replaced with M7 Priests and Sextons as they became available. Despite its limitations, the Bishop did provide a useful capability to the British in North Africa in the period before better self-propelled guns were available.

C: CARDEN-LOYD TANKETTE

The term "Carden-Loyd tankette" actually refers to a series of vehicles which were developed in the inter-war years. The Mark VI was the most successful, being built under licence in many countries.

In 1925, Carden-Loyd Tractors Ltd, a company owned by Sir John Carden and Vivian Loyd, created the Carden-Loyd One-Man Tankette. The idea was developed, and from the Mark IV onwards, became a two-man vehicle. The vehicles showed enough promise that Vickers bought Carden-Loyd Tractors in 1928. The Mark VI tankette became a great success, with over 300 seeing service in the British army, and more sold abroad. In the British army, the tankette saw service primarily as a machine gun carrier, but it was also used as a light gun tractor and mortar carrier.

It later formed the basis of the British Universal Carrier. Several other countries used it as a basis for development of their own tankette designs. Five Dutch Carden-Loyd tankettes saw action in Crete, fighting German paratroopers in May 1940.

D: DEERHOUND

The T17 (named Deerhound by the British) was an armoured car built in the US during World War II. Originally intended for service with both the British and US armies, in the end, neither army adopted it. The 250 vehicles that had been built had their armament (one 37mm gun and two machine guns) removed, and were used by the US Army Military Police Corps in the US.

The vehicle was designed by Ford in 1941 in response to a US Army Ordnance requirement for a medium armoured car. It had six wheels, all of which were driven. At the time, the British army was looking for medium and heavy armoured cars for service in North Africa. Production started in late 1942, but tests early the next year showed that the competing T17E1 design from Chevrolet was superior. Consequently, Britain decided to buy the T17E1 (which they named the Staghound), and the US army adopted the light M8 Greyhound armoured car.

E: EIFV

The EIFV is the Egyptian Infantry Fighting Vehicle, an interesting hybrid of an M113 armoured personnel carrier mated with a turret from an M2 Bradley infantry fighting vehicle. It was developed by BAE Systems for the Egyptian Ministry of Defence, with design starting in 1995, and production starting two years later.

The M113 chassis is enlarged, with an extra road wheel. The armour is improved to a point where it is proof against 14.5mm AP rounds in all aspects. A more powerful engine is fitted, to compensate for the extra weight caused by the additional armour and turret. It has a crew of three, and can carry seven infantrymen. A standard Bradley turret is fitted on top of the M113 hull, armed with a 25mm chain gun, coaxial 7.62mm machine gun, and twin launcher for TOW anti-tank missiles.

The combination of M113 hull and Bradley turret makes for a cheap and reasonably effective infantry fighting vehicle. The upgraded engine allows the vehicle to keep pace with the Egyptian army's M1A1/M1A2 Abrams MBTs.

F: FOX

Theoretically, there are many choices for "F", since the British army gives its armoured vehicles an FV designation. The Fox armoured car, for example, is more formally known as "FV721 Fox Combat Vehicle Reconnaissance (Wheeled)". However, choosing something like "FV4034 Challenger 2" would have felt like cheating, so I've gone for the Fox. Introduced in 1973, it served with the British army for about 20 years.

It has a crew of three (commander, gunner, and driver). The commander and gunner are seated in the turret, which is armed with a 30mm RARDEN cannon and a coaxial 7.62mm machine gun. The driver sits in the centre front of the hull. The vehicle has aluminium alloy armour sufficient to protect from small arms, but not from 0.50″/12.7mm HMG fire. The Fox can swim with the aid of a flotation screen, which takes about two minutes to erect, and can be dropped by parachute.

G: GVOZDIKA

The 2S1 Gvozdika self-propelled 122mm howitzer was accepted for service with the Soviet army in 1970 and began volume production in 1971. The hull is made of welded steel, based on the automotive components and running gear of the MT-LB. The driver sits at the front with the engine behind him, and the turret and fighting compartment at the rear. Within the turret, the commander sits on the left, with the gunner below and in front of him, and the loader to the right. The gun has sights for indirect and direct fire. A rate of fire of 5-8 rounds per minute can be maintained for a protracted period. 40 rounds of ammunition are carried in the vehicle, but standard practice during a fire mission would be for ammunition to be supplied from outside.

An odd feature of the Gvozdika is that the suspension can be adjusted to make the vehicle shorter, useful when transporting the vehicle by air. The standard tracks are 400mm wide, but like the MT-LB, 670mm wide tracks can be fitted for use in snow, swampy ground, etc. The 2S1 has NBC protection, infra-red driving lights, and a small infra-red searchlight on the commander's cupola. It is fully amphibious, propelled in the water by its tracks. Before entering the water, a bilge pump is switched on, shrouds are fitted to the hull front, water deflectors are lowered at the rear, the trim vane is erected at the front of the hull, and covers are fitted around the engine air intakes. Only 30 rounds are carried when swimming; any excess have to be removed before entering the water.

H: HORNET

The FV1620 Humber Hornet was an early ATGM carrier, which mounted two Malkara missiles on a Humber Pig APC. The missiles were carried on a retractable boom at the rear, which was lowered for transport, and elevated for firing. A pair of reload missiles were also carried. Developed to provide airborne forces with an anti-tank capability, it could be parachuted from a Blackburn Beverley transport aircraft.

The Malkara missile was controlled by the operator

using a small joystick, with guidance commands transmitted down a wire. Like other first-generation missiles, it was difficult to control, resulting in a low hit probability. However, it had a very large warhead, and could destroy any vehicle in service at the time it was introduced. Unusually, it had a HESH (High Explosive Squash Head) warhead, rather than the more common HEAT (High Explosive Anti-Tank).

The Hornet served with the British army from 1958 until the 1970s, when it was replaced by the Ferret Mark 5, a variant of the Ferret armoured car fitted with Swingfire anti-tank missiles.

I: INFANTERIKANONVAGN 91

The Infanterikanonvagn 91 is a Swedish tank destroyer that entered service in 1975. Designed to be highly mobile, it is lightly armoured (only able to withstand hits from guns of up to 20mm calibre on its frontal arc), and armed with a 90mm gun and two 7.62mm machine guns. It is fully amphibious, propelled in the water by its tracks, with some production models being fitted with propellers.

The driver sits in the front left of the hull, with the other three crew members in the turret. A hatch was added to the cramped turret to expel spent shell casings. Wide tracks and a powerful engine led to excellent cross-country performance and a top speed of 65km/hour (40mph).

Production ended in 1978, with a little over 200 vehicles being produced. Later, the vehicles were improved with the addition of a laser rangefinder, a thermal sleeve for the main gun, smoke grenade dischargers. In the early 1990s, Hägglunds proposed a new version with a 105mm main gun, and a version armed with an anti-tank guided missile. Neither went into production, however.

J: JAGUAR

The Jaguar 1 and Jaguar 2 are West German ATGM-armed tank destroyers, also known as Raketenjagdpanzer 3 and Raketenjagdpanzer 4, respectively. They were conversions of earlier tank destroyers. The Jaguar 1 was converted from the Raketenjagdpanzer 2, with the SS.11 ATGM replaced by a HOT ATGM. The Jaguar 2 was converted from the Kanonenjagdpanzer. The gun was removed, and a TOW AGTM launcher was fitted to the roof. Both vehicles had upgraded armour, a 7.62mm MG3 on an AA mounting and smoke dischargers. The Jaguar 1 also had a bow-mounted MG3.

Even with the additional armour, neither vehicle was heavily armoured, and so rely primarily for defence on speed and their low profile. They have an excellent top speed of 70 km/h (44 mph), and an operational range of around 400 km (250 miles). Both vehicles have a crew of four, all of whom sit in a fighting compartment to the front of the vehicle.

K: KANGAROO

The Kangaroo was an early armoured personnel carrier, created by simply removing the turret from a tank or (as in the photograph above), by removing the main armament from a self-propelled gun. It was devised by the Canadians as a way to reduce infantry losses. The first examples were based on M7 Priest self-propelled guns, converted at a field workshop code-named Kangaroo (which is where the name came from). As well as removing the main armament, the Priests had their front aperture covered over.

Most Kangaroos were based on Priests (these examples were sometimes referred to as "defrocked Priests") and Canadian Ram tanks, although Sherman and Churchill tanks were also used. All variants were known as Kangaroos, with the base vehicle name as a prefix (Sherman Kangaroo, Ram Kangaroo, Churchill Kangaroo, etc). Despite being created as a simple and quick solution to a problem, the Kangaroo was a great success, and many more conversions were carried out. The success of the Kangaroo led directly to post-war APCs such as the American M113, British FV432, and Soviet BTR-50.

L: LIGHT TANK, MARKS I TO VI

Although "light tank" can be a generic term, in this case it refers to the series of light tanks (Marks I to VI) produced by Vickers for the British Army in the inter-war period. I'm not including the Mark VII Tetrarch or Mark VIII Harry Hopkins, as they were significantly different from the earlier versions, and would warrant separate posts.

The Mark I Light Tank was developed from a design by Carden-Loyd, by then part of Vickers-Armstrong. Only about 9 or 10 were built, but experience gained was used in development of the Mark II, and then the Mark III and Mark IV. These first four versions were armed with a single 0.303″ Vickers machine gun, and had around 14mm of armour. The Mark V added a 0.50″ Vickers machine gun, giving the tank some measure of capability against other light tanks, and increased the crew from two to three (commander, gunner, and driver). The additional crewman made this version significantly more effective, since the commander was freed from having to operate the gun and radio.

The Mark VI was the only version produced in significant numbers, with production running to 1,682 vehicles. The Mark VIA and Mark VIB variants had the same armament as the Mark V, but the Mark VIC increased armament again to one 15mm Besa machine gun and one 7.92mm Besa machine gun.

All models saw were widely used for imperial policing duties in the British Empire, particularly India. When war broke out in 1939, more than 80% of the British Army's tanks were Mark VI Light Tanks. Most tanks used by the BEF during the Battle of France in 1940 were Mark VI Light Tanks, and they made up more than half the tank strength during the battles against the Italians in North Africa during 1940. Mark VI Light Tanks also fought in the battles of Greece and Crete.

M: MAUS

The Maus was a World War II German tank design, the result of a May 1942 demand from Hitler for an "indestructable" super-heavy tank. Most German generals considered the project a waste of time and resources, but Hitler had something of an obsession with "wonder weapons" of all types. The original plan was that a prototype, weighing around 100 tons, would be ready by mid 1943. In May 1943, a wooden mockup was ready, and presented to Hitler. By this time, the projected weight had increased to 188 tons. Maus' tracks were driven by electric motors, which in turn were powered by a large diesel engine coupled to an electrical generator.

A turretless prototype was ready by the end of 1943, and tests were carried out with a mock turret. The extreme weight meant that Maus could not cross bridges, and so an alternative solution had to be developed. Its huge size meant that it could ford relatively deep rivers. For others, a snorkel was developed that allowed it to cross rivers up to 45′ (13m) deep – when snorkelling, a second Maus would provide electrical power through a cable. Maus was armed with a 128mm gun, with a 75mm co-axial gun and a 7.92mm machine gun. Speed was only 8.1mph, with a range of 99 miles on roads, dropping to 39 miles off roads.

At the end of the war, the hull of the second prototype was extensively damaged, but the turret was relatively intact. The Soviets fitted the turret from the second proto-type to the hull of the first prototype, and carried out testing on this configuration. Once the testing was complete, it was moved to Kubinka Tank Museum, where it is still on public display.

N: NAHUEL

The Nahuel ("Tiger" in Mapuche, an aboriginal langauge) was an Argentinian World War II medium tank, designed in 1943. Although the design was indigenous, it was influenced by the US M4 Sherman. It was armed with a 75mm gun, with co-axial 12.7mm machine gun, and three hull-mounted 7.65mm machine guns. Its armour was up to 80mm thick, and well sloped. It had a top speed of 25mph and a range of 150 miles.

Production stopped after only sixteen vehicles had

been built, as in 1946 Argentina bought cheap M4 Shermans from the US and UK, some of which were the British Firefly variant, mounting 17 pounder guns.

O: OT-64

The OT-64 is a wheeled armoured personnel carrier, developed in the late 1950s and early 1960s as a joint project between Poland and Czechoslovakia. It is similar in concept and design to the Soviet BTR-60, but with some important differences. The OT-64 had overhead armour protection, had twin rear doors for entry and exit, and was powered by a single diesel engine. Like the BTR-60, it was air-portable and amphibious.

The original versions were not armed, but were later

equipped with 7.62mm or 12.7mm machine guns, some with an armoured shield fitted around the machine gun. These early models could carry 18 men in addition to the two crew. The later OT-64A was fitted with a small turret, mounting 14.5mm and 7.62mm machine guns. Later, some vehicles had the 14.5mm machine gun replaced with a 12.7mm NSV anti-aircraft machine gun. The turret reduced the troop carrying capacity to eight.

All models were fitted with NBC protection, night vision equipment, and a central tyre pressure regulation system, allowing the driver to control tyre pressure whilst driving. They have a top speed of around 60mph, and a range of 440 miles.

P: PIG

The Pig was a simple wheeled armoured personnel carrier, created by fitting an armoured body to a four-wheel drive 1-ton Humber truck. It was intended to be used only as an interim vehicle, until purpose-built APCs were available. However, when the British Army was deployed to Northern Ireland at the start of the Troubles, some form of armoured transport vehicle was needed. The Pig was deemed ideal for this purpose, since it in no way resembles a tank – it simply looks like what it is, an armoured truck.

As the Troubles continued, a Mark II version of the Pig was introduced. This had improved armour and heavy duty bull bars for breaking through barricades. Other specialised variants were created for use in Northern Ireland: the "Flying Pig" had fold-out riot screens on the sides and roof. The "Holy Pig" had a roof hatch surrounded by a perspex screen. The "Kremlin Pig" had wire screens for protection against shaped charges (particularly the RPG-7). The "Squirt Pig" was fitted with a water cannon. The "Foaming Pig" had a foam generator to minimise the effect of explosive devices. The "Felix Pig" was modified for use by use by Explosive Ordnance Disposal (EOD) teams.

The Pig was also used as the base vehicle for the Hornet, an earlier entry in this series.

Q: AL-QASWA LOGISTICS VEHICLE

I have to admit that finding an entry for Q was a challenge, and as it is, I haven't been able to find a picture of the Al-Qaswa under a licence that allows me to use it here. There are some good pictures on the PakDef Military Consortium site, however.

The Al-Qaswa is a tracked vehicle with a fully enclosed armoured crew compartment, and an open cargo bed to the rear. It is based on a lengthened M113P chassis, with an extra road wheel on each side, sharing many components with the M113P. Rather than an armoured personnel carrier used to carry supplies, it is specifically designed to transport supplies across all types of terrain. It is designed and built by Heavy Industries Taxila (HIT) in Pakistan.

It has a crew of two, and can carry up to six tons of cargo. A tarpaulin can be used to protect the cargo from inclement weather. HIT suggest that the vehicle could form the basis for a number of further vehicles, such as a missile launcher, ambulance, command vehicle, etc.

R: ROLLS-ROYCE ARMOURED CAR

The Royal Naval Air Service (RNAS) created the first British armoured car squadron in September 1914, requisitioning all Rolls-Royce Silver Ghost chassis for the new vehicle. The design had a fully armoured body with a rotating turret, mounting a single water-cooled Vickers 0.303″ machine gun. The first vehicles were delivered in December 1914, but by then the Western Front had moved to trench warfare, which armoured cars were ill-suited for.

The RNAS formed six armoured car squadrons, each

having twelve vehicles. Initially, one went to France and one to Africa to fight in the German colonies. Later, two squadrons were sent to Gallipoli. In August 1915 the RNAS squadrons were disbanded, and the material handed over to the army. The squadron in France was moved to Egypt, where the conditions were more suitable. T.E. Lawrence (more famously known as "Lawrence of Arabia") used a squadron of nine armoured cars in his campaign against the Turks, and rated them highly, saying that they were "more valuable than rubies".

Thirteen vehicles were given to the Irish Free State by the British government for use against the Irish Republican Army during the Irish Civil War. They were found to be very useful for convoy protection, and were used in the retaking of Waterford and Cork. They remained in service with the Irish army until 1944.

The armoured cars were modernised in 1920 and 1924, and in 1940, some vehicles had the turret replaced with an open-topped turret, mounting a Boys anti-tank rifle, Bren machine gun and smoke grenade launchers. 76 vehicles were in service with the British army when World War II broke out. They saw service in the Western Desert, Iraq, and Syria, but had been replaced by newer vehicles by the end of 1941.

S: SEXTON

By 1942, the British army in North Africa had decided that it needed self-propelled guns, and the hastily-created Bishop self-propelled 25 pounder wasn't good enough. They had adopted the American M7 Priest, but this was a logistical nightmare, since they were the only vehicles in British service that used a 105mm gun. What the British army really wanted was something like the Priest, but with a 25 pounder instead of a 105mm gun.

The Canadians supplied the answer. They mounted a 25 pounder gun-howitzer on the hull of a Ram tank (Canadian copy of the M3), in a similar mounting to that used on the Priest. After trials, the Canadian government ordered 124 vehicles, and the vehicle was designated "Sexton" in May 1943. Following trials in the UK, the British government ordered 300 vehicles, although these were to be built on the hulls of Grizzly tanks (Canadian copy of the M4A1 Sherman). To distinguish between the two, the Ram-based vehicles were designated Sexton Mark I, and the Grizzly-based vehicles were Sexton Mark II. A Sexton GPO (Gun Position Officer) variant was also built. This had no gun, but an extra radio, map tables, etc, and was used to direct artillery fire.

With the Sexton, the British army finally had a self-propelled 25 pounder that it was happy with. Sextons saw combat in Italy and north-western Europe, including the D-Day landings. It remained in British service until 1956.

T: TIGER

The Panzerkampfwagen VI Tiger Ausf E might be an obvious choice, but it's such an iconic vehicle that I decided it deserved a place.

The Tiger was developed in response to Soviet tank designs such as the T-34 and KV-1, which took the Germans by surprise when they invaded in 1941. The Tiger had significantly increased firepower and armour compared to previous vehicles, which led to a dramatic increase in weight to 54 tonnes. This increased weight put a great deal of strain on the automotive components, leading to an increased rate of breakdowns.

The 88mm gun already had a fearsome reputation among Allied tank crews, and the combination of that gun with thick armour (100-120mm at the front) led to the Tiger being feared and respected. The Sherman's 75mm gun could not penetrate the Tiger's frontal armour at any range, and could only penetrate the side armour from 100m. The British 17 pounder, as fitted in the Sherman Firefly, could penetrate the frontal armour at 1,000m range.

1,347 Tigers were built (by comparison, over 8,500 Panzer IV and around 6,000 Panthers were produced), but the Tiger had a disproportionate psychological impact on those who encountered it. In Western Europe, it was common for any tank sighting to be reported as a Tiger, despite the relatively low number of Tigers compared to other German tanks.

U: URUTU

The EE-11 Urutu is a wheeled, 6×6 armoured personnel carrier developed by Engesa of Brazil, and shares many components with the EE-9 Cascavel armoured car. Production began in 1974, and it was adopted by the Brazilian armed forces. It can carry 12 men in addition to the two crew, and it is amphibious, driven by a propeller when in the water. Production stopped in 1987, but the Brazilian vehicles have been upgraded since then, pending replacement by the new VBTP-MR.

The Urutu has been widely exported, and served as the base vehicle for several variants. It has a top speed of 55mph and a range of 530 miles. Armour is up to 12mm thick, and it is normally armed with a 12.7mm machine gun.

V: VALENTINE

The Valentine tank (officially the Tank, Infantry, Mk III, Valentine) was a British World War II infantry tank. It entered service in 1940, and proved to be a very reliable design. It saw combat in North Africa, Madagascar, the Pacific and in Russia (over three thousand were supplied to the Soviet Union under a lend-lease arrangement).

Originally armed with a 2-pounder gun, later versions had a 6-pounder or 75mm main gun. The Valentine was used as a basis for several variants, some of which were only used experimentally. These included a DD (Duplex Drive) version, primarily used for training, a CDL (Canal Defence Light) version, an observation post, mine clearers, bridging tanks, and flame throwers.

W: WIESEL

The Wiesel Armoured Weapons Carrier is a small, light vehicle, produced in several different variants. It was developed by Porsche during the 1970s to fulfill a West German Bundeswehr requirement for an air-transportable vehicle that could fight enemy tanks and infantry. The Bundeswehr cancelled funding in 1978, but Porsche continued development privately. The vehicle was accepted into Bundeswehr service in the 1980s. Trials of dropping the vehicle by parachute were unsuccessful, and so it is deployed by transport aircraft or helicopter.

The Wiesel's armour is proof against small arms and

shell splinters, although its small size and fast speed (43mph) provide some protection. There are several variants of the Wiesel, the most common being the fire support vehicle (armed with a 20mm cannon), and the TOW ATGM carrier.

Wiesel 2 entered service with the German army in 2001. This is longer and larger than Wiesel 1, and has better protection, including NBC protection. Like Wiesel 1, it has several variants, including an APC (carrying four men in addition to the crew), HOT ATGM carrier, and mortar carrier (mounting a 120mm mortar). A more powerful engine means that, despite its greater size and weight, maximum speed remains the same.

X: X1 LIGHT TANK

Like Q, X is something of a challenge. Luckily, however, the Brazilians built the X1 light tank. During World War II, Brazil received around 220 M3 light tanks from the US. By the 1970s, these vehicles were still being used, but maintenance had become a serious issue, and it was decided to modernise them. Two prototypes were converted in the early 1970s. These had new armour, engine, and suspension. The turret was replaced with a French turret mounting a 90mm gun.

The Brazilian army ordered 100 M3A1 tanks to be rebuilt as X1s. These were delivered between 1975 and 1978 and saw service with cavalry regiments until being withdrawn in the 1990s.

Y: YERAMBA

The Australian Regular Army was formed in 1947, and was to include armoured formations. Experience in World War II had shown that armoured units needed armoured, self-propelled artillery. It was soon found impossible to purchase modern self-propelled artillery from abroad, so a domestic solution was sought. The Yeramba was based on the Canadian Sexton Mark I, which mounted a 25 pounder on a Canadian copy of the M3 Grant medium tank. The Yeramba had M4 Sherman type suspension units, rather than those of the M3. 104 rounds of ammunition were carried, 16 armour piercing, the rest split between high explosive and smoke.

One prototype was built in 1949 and used for trials, and conversion of a further 13 started in 1950. Like the Sexton, the Yeramba was a simple but effective solution, and made logistical support easier, since both the M3 and the 25 pounder were standard equipment in the Australian army. All 14 vehicles were issued to the 22nd Field Regiment, Royal Australian Artillery, and remained in service until the regiment was disbanded in 1957. When the regiment was disbanded, the Yeramba was declared obsolete, and the vehicles disposed of.

Z: ZSU-57-2

The ZSU-57-2 entered service in 1955, providing the Warsaw Pact armies with a self-propelled anti-aircraft gun that could accompany the advancing armies.

The hull is based on a lightened T-54 chassis. The armour is much lighter and it has four road wheels instead of the T-54's five. Two air-cooled 57mm S-68 guns are fitted in a large, boxy, open-topped turret. 300 rounds of ammunition are carried, in a mix of armour-piercing, fragmentation-incendiary, and fragmentation, all of which had tracer. A tarpaulin cover is provided for protection against inclement weather.

The turret has powered traverse and elevation. Unlike the later and more successful ZSU-23-4, the ZSU-57-2 has no radar. This effectively means that it's use is limited to clear weather conditions. It has optical sights (initially with no rangefinder, though a rangefinder was later added), which are configured to allow use in a secondary role as a ground support vehicle. Maximum effective range of the guns is around 4,000m. Armour thickness is between 8 and 15mm, and the vehicle has a top speed of 31mph, with a range of 260 miles.

Obviously, this is the last of the AFV Alphabet series. It was interesting to research and write, I hope it was also interesting to read. My thanks to Tim Gow for the inspiration.

ABOUT RUSSELL PHILLIPS

Russell Phillips writes military history and RPG books. Born and brought up in a mining village in South Yorkshire, they have lived and worked in South Yorkshire, Lincolnshire, Cumbria and Staffordshire. Russell has always had a deep interest in history and conflicts all over the world, and enjoys sharing their knowledge with others through clear, factual accounts which shine a light on events of the past.

Their articles have been published in *Miniature Wargames*, *Wargames Illustrated*, *The Wargames Website*, and the Society of Twentieth Century Wargamers' *Journal*. They have been interviewed on WW2TV, BBC Radio Stoke, The WW2 Podcast, and Cold War Conversations. They currently live in Stoke-on-Trent with their wife and two children.

To get advance notice of new books, join Russell's mailing list at www.RussellPhillips.uk/list. You can leave at any time.

 twitter.com/RPBook

 facebook.com/RussellPhillipsBooks

youtube.com/RussellPhillipsBooks

ALSO BY RUSSELL PHILLIPS

- A Strange Campaign: The Battle for Madagascar
- A Ray of Light: Reinhard Heydrich, Lidice, and the North Staffordshire Miners
- Operation Nimrod: The Iranian Embassy Siege
- The Bear Marches West: 12 Scenarios for 1980s NATO vs Warsaw Pact Wargames
- A Fleet in Being: Austro-Hungarian Warships of WWI
- A Damn Close-Run Thing: A Brief History of the Falklands War
- This We'll Defend: The Weapons and Equipment of the U.S. Army

Weapons and Equipment of the Warsaw Pact

1. Tanks and Combat Vehicles of the Warsaw Pact
2. Combat Engineering Equipment of the Warsaw Pact
3. Artillery of the Warsaw Pact

Compendium: Weapons and Equipment of the Warsaw Pact: Volume One

Fiction

- The Bear's Claws: A Novel of World War III

RPG Books

- The Newspaper: A SHGGFTAWSGDSSFDF Delivery
- The Epiphany Club and the Great Library of Alexandria

IMAGE CREDITS

- ZSU-57-2 (entry and cover): User:VargaA, CC BY-SA 4.0 <https://creativecommons.org/licenses/by-sa/4.0>, via Wikimedia Commons

Printed in Great Britain
by Amazon